'Journey to the Depths: Angels and Demons'

Adams past

Journey to the Depths: Angels and Demons

The Impact Chronicles, Volume 5

Paul Smith

Published by Paul Smith, 2024.

JOURNEY TO THE DEPTHS: ANGELS AND DEMONS

First edition. February 26, 2024.

ISBN: 979-8224192274

Written by Paul Smith.

Also by Paul Smith

The Impact Chronicles
Seeds of Change: A Journey to Ramsey
Roots of Resilience: Nurturing Change
Rising Tide: The Rebirth of Ramsey
Seeds of Renewal: Love's Everlasting Bloom
Journey to the Depths: Angels and Demons

Watch for more at wix.pbsmith17@wix.com.

Table of Contents

Journey to the Depths: Angels and Demons'

is a captivating tale of love, resilience, and the indomitable spirit of the human heart. Through the depths of despair and the heights of joy, Adam and Emily's story serves as a testament to the transformative power of love, reminding us that even in the darkest of times, love will always prevail." Set against the breathtaking backdrop of the ocean, this tale follows Adam and Emily as they navigate the challenges of life's currents, united by their shared passion for marine biology and the wonders of the sea.

As Adam grapples with past traumas and struggles with his inner demons, Emily emerges as a beacon of light, guiding him towards healing and redemption. Together, they stand as guardians of the sea, embarking on a mission to protect and preserve its fragile ecosystems.

Amidst the trials and tribulations of their journey, Adam and Emily discover the true power of love, forging a connection that transcends time and space. Their bond deepens as they confront the darkness within themselves and embrace the light of hope and renewal.

In a triumph of love conquers all, Adam and Emily exchange vows of eternal devotion, laying the foundation for the love story that will unfold in 'Seeds of Change.' Their journey serves as a testament to the enduring power of love and the transformative impact it has on the human spirit.

'Journey to the Depths: Angels and Demons' is a captivating prequel that will transport readers on a journey, offering a glimpse into the origins of love and the seeds of change that will shape the future."

Adam's Past

Chapters

Title: "Journey to the Depths: Angels and Demons"

Chapter 1: A Meeting of Souls

The lecture hall hummed with anticipation as Adam slipped into a seat near the back, his mind buzzing with excitement. Tonight's lecture on marine conservation promised to be enlightening, a welcome distraction from the tumultuous thoughts swirling in his mind.

Adam's gaze drifted over the crowd, lingering on the vibrant sea of faces. He couldn't shake the lingering memories of past relationships that still haunted him, like shadows creeping at the edges of his consciousness. Lilith, with her seductive charm, had once held his heart in her grasp, leading him down a path of temptation and betrayal. And then there was Eve, the fiery redhead who had captured his soul with her unwavering love and devotion. Their tumultuous relationship had ended in heartache and regret, leaving Adam adrift in a sea of uncertainty.

But tonight was different. Tonight, Adam was determined to leave the ghosts of his past behind and embrace the promise of a new beginning. With each passing moment, he felt a glimmer of hope stirring within him, a sense of possibility that he hadn't felt in years. It was to pursue his dreams and find his playground again.

As the speaker took the stage, Adam refocused and leaned forward, eager to lose himself in the discussion. The speaker's passion and knowledge for marine conservation was palpable, her words echoing like a siren's call in the depths of his soul. He found himself nodding along, captivated by her knowledge and conviction.

Just as the lecture reached its crescendo, a tiny voice broke through this attention, pulling Adam from his reverie. He turned to see this beautiful woman standing beside him, her eyes alight with curiosity but dimmed in shame as her lateness was obvious, but this didn't bother Adam as he smiled forgetting the lectures last words.

"Excuse me, is this seat taken?" she asked softly, as a warm smile playing at the corners of her lips.

Adam shook his head, a faint smile tugging at his own lips. "No, not at all, it's all yours," he replied, gesturing to the empty chair beside him.

She thanked him and settled into the seat, her presence casting a warmth that chased away the lingering shadows of his past. "I'm Emily," she said, extending her hand in greeting.

"Adam," he replied, returning the gesture. "Nice to meet you, Emily, you haven't missed much,"

Their attention for knowledge was apparent between them as they listened eagerly to the lectures words of a hopeful future, with our students of today there will be a better tomorrow." echoed in the hall after she had left. This left Adam and Emily enthralled and energised to make their difference so they stayed seated for a little while talking about the lecturer and how if they could make a difference what would your dreams be. As they pondered this idea they smiled as they knew they couldn't possibly make that much of an impact but together their ideas could.

Their conversation flowed effortlessly as they discussed their shared love for the ocean. Adam was struck by Emily's passion and knowledge, feeling a connection unlike any he'd experienced before. It was as if fate had brought them together, guiding them towards each other in a sea of uncertainty. Their dreams and goals seemed to be aligned for once.

As the lecture lights drew to a close, Adam realised he didn't want their connection to end that night. He hesitated for a moment before gathering his courage. "Would you like to grab a coffee?" he asked, his heart racing with anticipation.

Emily's smile widened, her eyes sparkling with excitement. "I'd love to," she said, and in that moment, Adam knew he'd found someone special. But Emily was a lone venturer who looked after herself growing up with brothers. Adam who she could help him navigate the tumultuous waters of anything as she was so strong for someone so little which he admired and wanted to learn more but he was worried his past would halt him again quickly discarded any fantasy of a spark between them but a natural love for their passions and desires to save the smallest of creatures on this planet. Maybe together they could make a difference and discover the beauty of a love that was truly meant to be found in the ocean.

Chapter 2: Tides of Friendship

The coffee shop bustled with activity as Adam and Emily settled into a cosy corner booth, their conversation flowing effortlessly like the gentle wave and flow of the ocean tide. With each passing moment, Adam found himself drawn deeper into Emily's world, captivated by her infectious enthusiasm and genuine warmth.

As they sipped their drinks, Emily shared stories of her own journey into the world of marine biology, recounting the countless hours spent exploring tide pools and observing marine life in its natural habitat. Adam listened intently, hanging on her every word, his own passion for the ocean reignited with each tale she told.

Before long, they were lost in a world of their own making, their laughter filling the air as they shared jokes and traded stories into the night. It was as if they had known each other for years, their connection transcending time and space.

In that moment, Adam knew he had found a kindred spirit in Emily, someone who shared his love for the ocean and understood the depths of his soul like no one else ever had before. With her by his side, he felt a sense of belonging he had never known before, a feeling that filled him with a sense of peace and contentment he hadn't felt in years.

As they knew they could not continue all night talking they exchanged numbers and bid each other goodnight and parted ways. Adam couldn't help but feel a sense of excitement and anticipation for the journey that lay ahead. With Emily by his side, he knew anything was possible, and he couldn't wait to see where the tides of friendship would take them next but he had to remind himself of his past failings first before he could ever love or trust again.

In the days that followed their serendipitous meeting at the coffee shop, Adam and Emily's bond deepened with each passing moment they found themselves chatting about tomorrow and the past was rarely brought up. With each new connection woven together by the threads of shared experiences and unspoken understanding their trust grew. Whenever they navigated the complexities of their pasts, they found solace in the comfort of each other's presence, forging a connection that transcended the barriers of time and circumstance as it was now that defines us but the past has taught us to grow.

Chapter 3: Echoes of the Past

As Emily confided in Adam about the trials she had endured, his heart ached with empathy for the pain she had suffered. He listened with a compassionate ear as she shared the story of a loss that had left her broken and scarred, the memory of a child she had loved and lost still haunting her dreams.

In Emily's eyes, Adam saw a depth of sorrow and resilience that touched his soul in ways he could scarcely comprehend. He marvelled at her strength, her unwavering determination to carry on in the face of unimaginable loss, and he knew then that she was a woman of extraordinary courage and grace. This is why he understood her passion to change and make a difference to world before it's too late and we are no longer here to do anything but rather than saying I didn't make a difference, their courage enthralled them to make a difference this time and show the next generations that love prevails over the darkness and hatred procured out by so many.

Together, they found light as they navigated the turbulent waters of grief and healing, finding solace in the simple act of being there for one another. In Adam, Emily found a pillar of strength, a source of comfort and support in her darkest hours. And in Emily, Adam found a kindred spirit, a soulmate whose presence brought light into the shadows of his own troubled past.

Days slipped into weeks as the pair grew in love for change and colour but currently where they live is grey and old. The old sea harbours lay empty like the bed and breakfasts as life seems to have disappeared and was forgotten. The couple knew staying there was not the long term dream.

As they embarked on their journey of friendship and discovery, Adam and Emily knew that they would always be there for each other no matter what out of respect, they were bound together by the unbreakable bonds of love and understanding forged in their playgrounds. They knew to make a difference would be to change but they needed to both explain this to their friends and families that their new found love and connection is special and they are taking time to get to learn on another. So as they faced the challenges of the future together, they took comfort in the knowledge that no matter what trials lay ahead, they would always have each other to lean on as they knew they could do anything together as their love grew.

Chapter 4: Guardians of the Sea

As Adam and Emily embarked on their journey of environmental activism, they realised the importance of garnering support and building a community around their cause. Leveraging Emily's online influence and social media presence, they launched a grassroots campaign to rally volunteers and raise awareness for their coastal conservation initiatives just as they once discussed all those weeks ago.

With Emily's adeptness in navigating the digital realm, they swiftly amassed a dedicated following of like-minded individuals who shared their passion for protecting the ocean. Through engaging content, powerful storytelling, and strategic outreach efforts, they inspired others to join their movement and lend their voices to the cause.

Their efforts bore fruit as volunteers poured in from all corners of the community, eager to lend a hand in cleaning up their coastal town and safeguarding its natural beauty for future generations. Together, they organised beach clean-ups, educational workshops, and advocacy events, leaving a lasting impact on their local environment and instilling a sense of pride and ownership in their fellow citizens around the town.

Word of their grassroots movement spread like wildfire, catching the attention of local media outlets eager to shine a spotlight on their inspiring story. Before long, Adam and Emily found themselves featured in the pages of the local newspaper and invited to share their journey on radio broadcasts, further amplifying their message and expanding their reach.

As their friends and family witnessed the impact of their collective efforts, they couldn't help but admire Adam and Emily's unwavering dedication and the deep connection that fueled their shared passion. With each clean-up event and community initiative, their bond grew stronger, a testament to the power of love and collaboration in creating positive change.

In the eyes of their loved ones, Adam and Emily were more than just partners—they were beacons of hope, leading the charge in a movement to protect the planet they called home. And as they looked towards the horizon, they knew that together, they could accomplish anything they set their minds to, for their love was not only a source of strength but also a catalyst for meaningful action and lasting change.

Chapter 5: Whispers of Temptation

With the newfound attention garnered by their coastal conservation initiatives, Adam found himself thrust into the spotlight in ways he had never imagined. As their grassroots movement gained momentum and their social media following swelled, Adam's resolve was put to the test as past temptations resurfaced, threatening to cast a shadow over his relationship with Emily. Emily's online presence was growing daily and she was attracting a lot of unnecessary attention that troubled the couple's new adventure as they needed this platform to make a difference in today's modern world. So they continued knowing not to believe everything is real online.

The whispers of temptation grew louder with each passing day, fueled by the lingering echoes of his tumultuous past with Lilith and Eve. Doubt crept into Adam's mind, clouding his judgement and stirring feelings of insecurity and inadequacy. He questioned whether he was worthy of the love and admiration he received from Emily and the community they had worked so hard to build but was this it. What about his dreams to build an Aquarium and Sea Life Gallery and leave his legacy.

Amidst the tumult of his inner turmoil, Emily remained a steadfast beacon of light, her unwavering support and understanding serving as a source of strength in Adam's darkest hours. She stood by his side, offering words of encouragement and reassurance, her love a constant reminder of the bond they shared and grew and the promise of a brighter future together somewhere new would be real one day when it was possible.

Despite the whispers of temptation that threatened to pull him astray, Adam knew deep down that his new found heart belonged to Emily and that their love was everything worth fighting for. With her love as his guiding light, he found the strength to confront his inner demons head-on, determined to overcome the obstacles that stood in their way and push aside any dark thought or temptation.

As the weeks passed, they faced the challenges of temptation and betrayal together from their closet of business friends but Adam and Emily emerged stronger than ever before, as their bond forged in the fires of adversity and tested by the trials of life. With each obstacle they conquered, their love grew deeper and more resilient, a beacon of hope amidst the darkness that threatened to consume them online and in spirit.

In the end, Adam's resolve remained unwavering, his commitment to Emily was stronger than ever before. And as they stood hand in hand, ready to face whatever challenges lay ahead next, they knew that they could do it together as their love was a force to be reckoned with, capable of overcoming even the greatest of obstacles.

Chapter 6: Angels Among Us

In moments of darkness, when the weight of the world seemed too heavy to bear, Adam and Emily found solace in the kindness and love of their friends and family. As they navigated the tumultuous waters of temptation and doubt, they drew strength from the unwavering support of those who stood by their side, ready to offer a helping hand or a listening ear whenever they needed it most.

However, amidst the newfound attention and praise for their coastal conservation initiatives, Adam and Emily also faced a darker side of humanity—one filled with jealousy and hatred. Threats and harassment flooded their online platforms, casting a shadow over their efforts to make the world a better place.

Confusion and hurt consumed them as they struggled to understand why people would be so cruel in the face of their good intentions. They found themselves questioning their purpose and doubting whether their actions were truly making a difference in a world plagued by negativity.

It was in these moments of despair that friends emerged as beacons of hope, offering words of encouragement and unwavering support to Adam and Emily. With their wise counsel and compassionate hearts, they helped them navigate the stormy seas of online harassment, reminding them that they were not alone in their fight for a better world.

Together, they leaned on each other for strength, drawing courage from the love and acceptance that surrounded them. In the embrace of their chosen family, Adam and Emily found the resilience to stand tall in the face of adversity, knowing that their angels would always be there to guide them towards the light.

And as they emerged from the darkness, stronger and more united than ever before, Adam and Emily knew that their journey was far from over. With their hearts set on a brighter future, they continued to spread love and kindness wherever they went, knowing that even in the darkest of times, there were angels among them, ready to lead them towards the promise of a better tomorrow.

Chapter 7: Dancing with Demons

As Adam and Emily journeyed deeper into their relationship not just in business, they found themselves confronting their innermost fears and insecurities. The scars of their past relationships still lingered, casting shadows of doubt and uncertainty over their newfound love together. Yet, with each passing day, they learned to embrace their vulnerabilities, knowing that true strength lay in facing their demons together.

Their bond grew stronger as they opened up to each other, sharing their deepest fears and insecurities without reservation. In the warmth of each other's embrace, they found solace and comfort, knowing that they were not alone in their struggles.

But just as they began to find peace in each other's arms, a familiar spectre from Adam's past reemerged, threatening to shatter the fragile peace they had worked so hard to build. Lilith and Narmah, driven by greed and selfishness, returned demanding more money for their upbringings, their presence casting a dark shadow over Adam and Emily's happiness.

Adam and Emily stood united against the demons of their past, refusing to let them tear them apart. With unwavering determination, they confronted Lilith and Narmah, standing firm in their resolve to protect the life they had built together.

Together, they faced their demons head-on, drawing strength from each other as they navigated the stormy seas of their past. And as they emerged victorious in agreement, they knew that their love was stronger than any obstacle they might face, a beacon of hope in the darkness that threatened to consume them in the future.

With Lilith and Narmah resigned once more to the shadows, Adam and Emily turned their gaze towards the future, ready to embrace whatever challenges lay ahead. For they knew that no matter what trials they might face, as long as they had each other, they could overcome anything. And as they danced with their demons, they did so hand in hand, their love guiding them through the darkness and into love.

Chapter 8: A Symphony of Love

As Adam and Emily continued to navigate the intricacies of their relationship, their trust deepened into a profound and abiding love. With each passing day, they discovered new depths to their connection, weaving a tapestry of intimacy and understanding that bound them together in an unbreakable bond.

In the quiet moments they shared, nestled in each other's arms, they found solace and comfort, their hearts beating in harmony as they revealed the beauty of their love. Their souls danced to the rhythm of their shared laughter and whispered promises, their love a symphony of joy and passion that echoed through the halls of their hearts.

Their closest friends and family looked on with excitement and joy as Adam and Emily embarked on this new chapter of their lives together. With hearts full of love and anticipation, they celebrated the beauty of their relationship, showering them with blessings and well-wishes as they set forth on their journey hand in hand.

As Adam and Emily gazed into each other's eyes, they knew that their love was a force to be reckoned with, a beacon of hope in a world filled with uncertainty. With each step they took together, they embraced the promise of a future filled with endless possibilities, knowing that as long as they had each other, they could conquer anything that came their way.

And as they stood on the threshold of a new beginning, surrounded by the love and support of their cherished loved ones, Adam and Emily knew that their love was not just a fleeting moment in time, but a timeless symphony that would echo through the ages, a testament to the power of love to conquer all.

Chapter 9: Overcoming Obstacles

Despite the setbacks and challenges that came their way, Adam and Emily remained steadfast in their commitment to each other and their shared goals. With unwavering determination, they faced life's storms head-on, like bills, the weather or even food and illness that threatened to derail their journey, weathering each obstacle together.

They sought out their new beginnings in the search of other coastal towns up and down the country, Adam and Emily found themselves drawn to the allure of the Isle of Man. Nestled in the middle of the Irish Sea, this majestic island beckoned to them like a beacon of hope, its shores teeming with natural beauty and rich history.

With hearts full of excitement and curiosity, Adam and Emily wasted no time in booking a trip to explore this enchanting destination for themselves. They were captivated by the promise of pristine beaches, rugged cliffs, and lush landscapes, all surrounded by a thriving marine ecosystem filled with pods of dolphins, humpback whales, seals, and basking sharks, perfect for their marine passions.

The Isle of Man spoke to their natural instincts, tugging at their heartstrings with its untamed wilderness and boundless beauty. They knew in their hearts that they had to go and see it for themselves, to immerse themselves in its natural splendour and uncover the secrets that lay hidden within its shores.

As they set foot on the island, Adam and Emily felt a sense of belonging wash over them, as if they had finally found a place where they could truly be themselves. Surrounded by the breathtaking scenery and the warm embrace of the island's inhabitants, they knew that they had stumbled upon something truly special. It was like walking around apart of Britain's history that has not been touched by the new world. With its ancient settlements and historic castles, the history teems out as you explore. Emily wasted no time in exploring the island's many wonders, from its historic buildings and quaint villages to its pristine rocky beaches and rugged coastline. They soon forged connections with the locals, learning about the island's rich cultural heritage and deep-rooted traditions as they shared in its culture Ellan Vannin Isle of Man.

And as they basked in the beauty of their surroundings, Adam and Emily knew that they had overcome every obstacle that had stood in their way, emerging stronger and more resilient than ever before. With the Isle of Man as their guiding light, they realised at that moment they have embarked on a new chapter of their lives together, ready to embrace whatever adventures lay ahead on their new home on the Isle of Man.

Chapter 10: Beyond the Horizon

As early spring painted the landscape with vibrant colours, Adam and Emily embarked on a journey to the Isle of Man, eager to explore its wonders and unravel the mysteries of its seven kingdoms. With hearts full of excitement and anticipation, they set foot on the island, ready to embrace the adventures that awaited them.

From the moment they arrived, Adam and Emily were enchanted by the beauty and charm of the Isle of Man. They wandered through its historic streets, marvelling at ancient castles and picturesque villages, each corner revealing a new layer of history and culture.

But as their short break came to an end, Adam and Emily found themselves reluctant to leave, their hearts longing for more time to explore this magical place. They knew that their journey was far from over, and they were determined to make the Isle of Man their home.

Upon their return, Adam and Emily wasted no time in searching for a place they could call their own on the island. They scoured local property listings and newspapers, hoping to find a home they could afford to buy or renovate. But the harsh realities of the economy made their dreams seem out of reach, forcing them to put their plans on hold once again.

Undeterred, Emily took to her laptop, channelling her passion and creativity into writing about their dreams and aspirations. With each word she typed, she captured the essence of their shared vision, painting a vivid picture of the life they hoped to build together on the Isle of Man.

Together, Adam and Emily weighed the pros and cons, carefully considering their options and the challenges they would face. Despite the uncertainties that lay ahead, they knew that their love and determination would see them through any obstacle.

And so, with courage and optimism in their hearts, Adam and Emily made the bold decision to put their house on the market, taking a leap of faith into the unknown. They knew that the road ahead would be filled with challenges and hardships, but they also knew that together, they could conquer anything that stood in their way.

As they embarked on this new chapter of their lives hand in hand, Adam and Emily looked towards the horizon with hope and excitement, ready to embrace the adventures that awaited them on the Isle of Man and beyond. For they knew that no matter what trials they may face, as long as they had each other, their love would light the way forward.

Chapter 11: Trials and Tribulation

As the year progressed, and the promise of a new beginning beckoned, Adam and Emily found themselves facing unforeseen challenges as the shadow of a global pandemic descended upon the world. What began as whispers of uncertainty soon turned into a deafening roar of fear and panic as COVID-19 spread like wildfire, disrupting lives and shattering dreams in its wake.

Gatherings and celebrations, once a source of joy and connection, became fraught with danger as the threat of the virus loomed large. Adam and Emily, like so many others, found themselves forced to retreat into isolation, their dreams of exploring the Isle of Man and building a new life together put on hold indefinitely.

The days stretched into weeks, and the weeks into months, as Adam and Emily navigated the turbulent waters of lockdowns and restrictions. Each day brought new challenges and hardships, testing the limits of their resilience and determination.

Yet, amidst the chaos and uncertainty, Adam and Emily refused to lose hope. They drew strength from their love for each other, finding solace in the knowledge that they were not alone in their struggles. Together, they weathered the storm, leaning on each other for support and encouragement as they faced the unknown.

As the world around them grappled with the devastating impact of the pandemic, Adam and Emily clung to the belief that better days were ahead. They dreamed of a future where they could once again roam freely, exploring the wonders of the world hand in hand.

As Adam and Emily grappled with the challenges of the pandemic, another storm brewed on the horizon, threatening to engulf them in its turmoil. Adam's father, already battling Parkinson's disease, saw his condition worsen as the months dragged on, making communication increasingly difficult and straining their family's bonds.

The once vibrant and lively conversations Adam shared with his father became a shadow of their former selves, as the disease robbed him of his ability to express himself. Each visit became a heartbreaking reminder of the toll Parkinson's was taking on their family, leaving Adam feeling helpless and lost in the face of his father's declining health.

Emily stood by Adam's side, offering unwavering support and comfort as he grappled with the emotional weight of his father's illness. Together, they navigated the complexities of caregiving, finding solace in each other's arms as they faced the uncertainties of the future.

Despite the challenges they faced, Adam and Emily refused to let despair consume them. They drew strength from their love for each other, finding moments of joy and connection amidst the darkness that threatened to overwhelm them.

As they watched Adam's father struggle with each passing day, Adam and Emily vowed to cherish the moments they shared with their loved ones, knowing that time was precious and fleeting. They leaned on each other for support, finding solace in the knowledge that they were not alone in their struggles.

And as the year drew to a close, Adam and Emily looked towards the horizon with cautious optimism, ready to face whatever challenges the new year might bring. For they knew that no matter what trials they may face, as long as they had each other, they could overcome anything that stood in their way. And together, they stood strong, united in their love and unwavering in their resolve to build a future filled with hope and possibility.

And as they faced the trials and tribulations that life threw their way, Adam and Emily clung to the hope that better days were ahead. They knew that their love was a beacon of light in the darkest of times, guiding them through the storm and leading them towards a brighter tomorrow. And together, they stood strong, united in their determination to weather the challenges that lay ahead, no matter what obstacles they may face.

Chapter 12: Farewell to a Father

As the pandemic tightened its grip on the world, Adam's longing to see his father grew with each passing day. Lockdown restrictions meant that visits were impossible, and the distance weighed heavily on Adam's heart. He yearned to hold his father's hand, to share a smile, to whisper words of love and reassurance in his ear. But fate had other plans.

In the midst of their separation, tragedy struck. Adam's father suffered a severe fall, landing him in the hospital with grave injuries. The news sent shockwaves through the family, leaving Adam reeling with grief and regret. He cursed the cruel hand fate had dealt them, lamenting the missed opportunities and moments lost to time that he never get back.

Despite Covids best efforts, Adam was able to be by his father's side in his final hours and moments. The confines of lockdown and the relentless march of the pandemic nearly made it impossible for him to say goodbye in person and he felt lucky as so many others did not get to say goodbye. Instead, they are left to grapple with the agony of separation, heart heavy with the weight of what could have been.

Emily stood by Adam's side, offering comfort and solace as he navigated the depths of his sorrow. Together, they mourned the loss of a beloved father, a pillar of strength and wisdom whose absence left a gaping hole in their lives especially at a time of family celebration.

In the quiet moments that followed, Adam found solace in memories of his father, holding onto the cherished moments they had shared together. He took comfort in the knowledge that his father's love would live on in his heart, a guiding light in the darkness that threatened to consume him and his dreams. In time, Adam was allowed to stay and comfort his Mother and arrange his father's funeral. It was challenging days compiling happy memories of this father's past but a celebration of a man who guided his children calmly into this future.

As Adam bid farewell to his father in those final days upto his funeral, he vowed to honour his memory by living each day to the fullest, cherishing the time he had with loved ones and never taking a moment for granted. And as he looked towards the future, he knew that his father would always be with him, a guardian angel watching over him from above.

Chapter 13: Embracing the Light

In the wake of Adam's father's passing, Adam and Emily found themselves enveloped in a haze of grief and sorrow. But amidst the darkness, a glimmer of hope emerged, beckoning them towards the light.

As a family, they made the decision to visit the Isle of Man in the springtime, seeking solace and renewal amidst the island's tranquil beauty. The promise of sun-kissed beaches and vibrant landscapes offered a welcome respite from their grief, a chance to heal and find joy once more.

With each passing day, Adam and Emily felt the weight of their sorrow begin to lift, replaced by a sense of peace and serenity. They reveal the simple pleasures of life, basking in the warmth of the sun and the gentle embrace of the ocean breeze.

Their online and ocean adventures, once a source of joy and excitement, had all but stopped since Adam's father's death. But as they explored the Isle of Man together, they felt a renewed sense of purpose and vitality coursing through their veins.

They wandered through quaint villages and ancient ruins, marvelling at the island's rich history and cultural heritage. They hiked along rugged cliffs and explored hidden coves, each step bringing them closer to the heart of the island and to each other.

In the midst of their adventures, Adam and Emily found themselves surrounded by the beauty of nature, the vibrant colours and fragrant blooms serving as a reminder of the endless cycle of life and renewal. They revelled in the magic of the moment, grateful for the opportunity to create new memories together as a family.

As they stood on the shores of the Isle of Man, watching the sun set over the horizon, Adam and Emily knew that their journey was far from over. But as long as they had each other, they were ready to face whatever challenges the future might bring, secure in the knowledge that love would light their way forward, illuminating even the darkest of nights.

Chapter 14: Realising the Dream

As Adam and Emily stood on the shores of the Isle of Man, basking in the beauty of their surroundings, they knew that their journey was far from over. The island had captured their hearts, and they longed to make it their home. But turning their dream into reality would require courage, determination, and a leap of faith.

With a newfound sense of purpose burning within them, Adam and Emily began to map out their plan for the future. They knew that moving their lives to the Isle of Man would require sacrifices and hard work, but they were willing to do whatever it took to make their dream a reality.

The first step was to sell everything they owned, from their house to their belongings, in order to fund their adventure. It was a daunting task, but Adam and Emily approached it with optimism and determination. They sorted through their possessions, deciding what to keep and what to let go of, each item carrying memories of a life they were preparing to leave behind.

As they watched their belongings disappear one by one, Adam and Emily felt a mix of excitement and apprehension wash over them. They were leaving behind the familiar comforts of home for the unknown possibilities of the future, and the journey ahead was filled with uncertainty.

But with each sale, they felt a weight lift from their shoulders, knowing that they were one step closer to their dream. They embraced the process of letting go, finding freedom in the simplicity of a life unencumbered by material possessions.

As they packed up their remaining belongings, Adam and Emily felt a sense of anticipation building within them. They were embarking on the adventure of a lifetime, and they couldn't wait to see where the road would take them.

With their hearts set on the Isle of Man, Adam and Emily took a leap of faith, trusting that the universe would guide them on their journey. They knew that the path ahead would be filled with challenges and obstacles, but they were ready to face them head-on, secure in the knowledge that together, they could overcome anything.

And so, with a sense of excitement and anticipation, Adam and Emily put their houses on the market, with their hearts filled with hope and their spirits soaring with the promise of a brighter tomorrow. They were ready to chase their dreams and carve out a new life for themselves on the shores of the Isle of Man, where adventure awaited at every turn.

Chapter 15: Embracing Farewell

As the day of departure drew near, Adam and Emily found themselves caught in a whirlwind of emotions. The prospect of leaving behind their loved ones filled them with a mix of excitement and sorrow, and they grappled with the weight of their impending farewell.

For Adam, the thought of saying goodbye to his daughters was a heavy burden to bear. Despite his efforts to maintain a connection with them, the distance between them seemed to widen with each passing day. He longed to be there for them, to witness their growth and share in their joys and sorrows. But as the time to leave drew near, he realised that he would have to find solace in the memories they had shared and the hope of reuniting in the future.

Meanwhile, Emily's family surrounded them with love and support, their laughter and warmth a soothing balm to their troubled hearts. They shared stories and reminisced about the adventures they had shared together, finding comfort in each other's presence as they prepared to say goodbye.

As they packed up their belongings and made final preparations for their journey, Adam and Emily found themselves overwhelmed by a sense of gratitude for the life they had lived and the people they had known. They knew that the road ahead would be challenging, filled with twists and turns, but they also knew that they were not alone.

With heavy hearts and tear-filled eyes, Adam and Emily bid farewell to the place they had called home, their memories and dreams packed away in boxes and suitcases. They knew that they were leaving behind a chapter of their lives, but they also knew that they were stepping into a new beginning, filled with endless possibilities and adventures yet to come as they couldn't wait to reconnect with their island friends David and Maria.

As they drove away from the familiar sights and sounds of their old life, Adam and Emily held hands tightly, drawing strength from each other's presence as they embarked on the journey ahead. They knew that the road would be long and winding, but they also knew that as long as they had each other, they could weather any storm.

And so, with hearts full of hope and determination, Adam and Emily set their sights on the horizon, ready to embrace whatever the future held in store. Together, they faced the unknown with courage and resilience, knowing that no matter where life took them, their love would light the way forward.

Adam and Emily -

Adam and Emily -

Series Title: The Impact Chronicles

Synopsis:

"The Impact Chronicles" is a series of interconnected stories that celebrate the

resilience, courage, and compassion of individuals striving to make a difference in

their communities and the world at large. Each instalment follows the journeys of

diverse characters as they navigate personal challenges, overcome obstacles, and

discover the transformative power of collective action.

In Book 1, "Seeds of Change: Stories of Hope and Resilience," readers are introduced

to the coastal town of Ramsey, where Maria, David, Emily, and Adam embark on a

quest to revitalise their community. Through their shared vision and unwavering

determination, they plant the seeds of change that inspire others to join them in their

mission to create a better future.

Book 2, "Roots of Resilience: Nurturing Change," delves deeper into the lives of the

residents of Ramsey as they confront economic hardships, environmental threats,

and personal struggles. Despite the odds, they draw strength from their roots and

work together to cultivate resilience, fostering a sense of belonging and

empowerment in their community.

In Book 3, "Echoes of Change: Shadows of the Past," Ramsey faces a new challenge when a devastating storm tests the town's resilience. As old wounds resurface and

tensions rise, the residents must confront the shadows of the past and find the

courage to rebuild and heal together, forging stronger bonds and deeper connections

in the process.

Book 4, "Seeds of Renewal: Love's Everlasting Bloom," shifts focus to Emily and

Adam as they navigate the complexities of love, loss, and renewal. Through their

journey, they discover that love has the power to heal wounds, ignite passions, and

inspire transformation, reminding them of the enduring hope that lies within each

new beginning.

Through its heartfelt narratives and compelling characters, "The Impact Chronicles"

explores the universal themes of compassion, resilience, and the profound impact of

small acts of kindness and courage. It serves as a testament to the indomitable

human spirit and the infinite possibilities that arise when individuals come together

to create positive change in the world.

Book 1

Title: Seeds of Change: A Journey to Ramsey

Summary:

In the first instalment of the "Seeds of Change" series, we follow the interconnected

stories of four individuals – Maria, David, Emily, and Adam – as they embark on a

journey to the coastal town of Ramsey in search of new beginnings.

Maria, a seasoned activist, arrives in Ramsey with a vision of creating community

gardens to promote food security and social cohesion. David, an environmental

engineer, sees Ramsey as an opportunity to implement green infrastructure projects

that will mitigate the effects of climate change and enhance the town's resilience.

Emily, a digital influencer, finds herself drawn to Ramsey's picturesque landscapes

and vibrant community spirit. With her online platform, she seeks to raise awareness

about local issues and inspire others to take action.

Adam, a marine biologist, is captivated by Ramsey's rich marine biodiversity and

sees potential in establishing a sea life sanctuary and tropical aquarium to educate

and engage visitors.

AS THESE FOUR INDIVIDUALS settle into Ramsey, they encounter challenges and setbacks

but also discover the power of community, resilience, and hope. Together, they plant the seeds of change that will transform Ramsey into a beacon of sustainability,

compassion, and renewal.

Through their journeys of self-discovery and collective action, Maria, David, Emily,

and Adam demonstrate that even in the face of adversity, ordinary individuals can

make an extraordinary impact when they come together with a shared purpose.

Let's go back to the beginning all those years ago.

The Impact Chronicles

Series Title: The Impact Chronicles
Synopsis:
"The Impact Chronicles" is a series of interconnected stories that celebrate the

resilience, courage, and compassion of individuals striving to make a difference in

their communities and the world at large. Each instalment follows the journeys of

diverse characters as they navigate personal challenges, overcome obstacles, and

discover the transformative power of collective action.

In Book 1, "Seeds of Change: Stories of Hope and Resilience," readers are introduced

to the coastal town of Ramsey, where Maria, David, Emily, and Adam embark on a

quest to revitalise their community. Through their shared vision and unwavering

determination, they plant the seeds of change that inspire others to join them in their

mission to create a better future.

Book 2, "Roots of Resilience: Nurturing Change," delves deeper into the lives of the

residents of Ramsey as they confront economic hardships, environmental threats,

and personal struggles. Despite the odds, they draw strength from their roots and

work together to cultivate resilience, fostering a sense of belonging and

empowerment in their community.

In Book 3, "Echoes of Change: Shadows of the Past," Ramsey faces a new challenge when a devastating storm tests the town's resilience. As old wounds resurface and

tensions rise, the residents must confront the shadows of the past and find the

courage to rebuild and heal together, forging stronger bonds and deeper connections

in the process.

Book 4, "Seeds of Renewal: Love's Everlasting Bloom," shifts focus to Emily and

Adam as they navigate the complexities of love, loss, and renewal. Through their

journey, they discover that love has the power to heal wounds, ignite passions, and

inspire transformation, reminding them of the enduring hope that lies within each

new beginning.

Through its heartfelt narratives and compelling characters, "The Impact Chronicles"

explores the universal themes of compassion, resilience, and the profound impact of

small acts of kindness and courage. It serves as a testament to the indomitable

human spirit and the infinite possibilities that arise when individuals come together

to create positive change in the world.

Book 1
Title: Seeds of Change: A Journey to Ramsey
Summary:
In the first instalment of the "Seeds of Change" series,

Adam's Past

Adam's Past

Adam's Past

The Impact Chronicles

Also by Paul Smith

The Impact Chronicles
Seeds of Change: A Journey to Ramsey
Roots of Resilience: Nurturing Change
Rising Tide: The Rebirth of Ramsey
Seeds of Renewal: Love's Everlasting Bloom
Journey to the Depths: Angels and Demons

Watch for more at wix.pbsmith17@wix.com.

About the Author

Paul smith Artist, Aurthor & Designer. Island resident since 1999
Read more at wix.pbsmith17@wix.com.